CHALLENGE

SOLDIER in training

David Orme

CONTENTS

Introduction 2

Fitness training 5

Drill 6

Fieldcraft 8

Map reading 10

Weapon training 12

First aid and defence 14

Recreation and initiative training 16

Military education and welfare advice 18

Officer training 20

Special training 22

Glossary 24

Acknowledgement
The author would like to thank the Aldershot Military Museum, Aldershot, Hampshire, for help in the preparation of this book.

INTRODUCTION

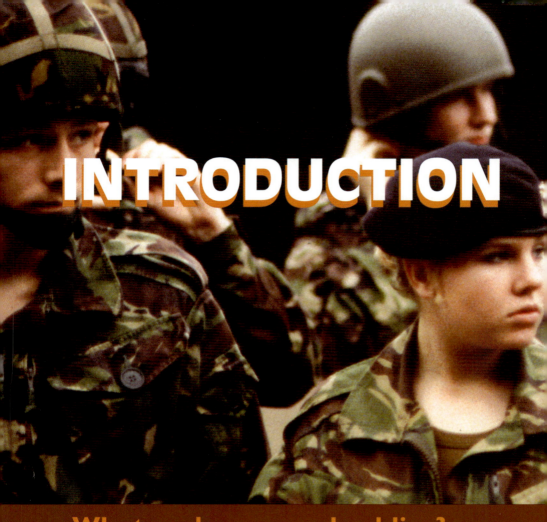

What makes a good soldier?

Soldiers need to be hard working and have plenty of common sense! It is important that they can work as a team, and obey orders. Senior soldiers called officers have to be good at giving orders.

Anyone who wants to be a soldier needs to be fit and have good eyesight. Recruits need to be tall enough to do all the duties of a soldier.

Training to be a soldier

Soldiers have a lot to learn in their basic training. Recruits will work hard on improving their fitness, and learn all about the job of a soldier. This book tells you about the hard work – and fun – of learning to be a soldier.

To find out more visit the army website:
www.army.mod.uk/army/recruit

FITNESS TRAINING

What does this mean?

If you are to be a good soldier you must be fit! You need to be able to walk and run carrying heavy weights. Recruits who are not fit enough have to work very hard to improve their fitness.

How fit do soldiers have to be?

The army checks the fitness of soldiers twice a year. Once they have warmed up, they have to do press-ups and sit-ups, then a run. All this has to be done in a fixed time. If they fail the test, they have to do extra training every morning.

DRILL

What does this mean?

Drill means marching in a group, **keeping in step** with each other.

What do soldiers have to learn?

They have to learn how to march, and to understand orders such as '**quick march**', '**attention!**' and '**stand at ease**'. They must learn to be smartly dressed, too.

What does the training involve?

First, recruits will learn how to march together. They must keep in time with each other and obey orders quickly. Then they will learn how to do **rifle** drill and march with a rifle. They must put up with being shouted at – until they get it right!

FIELDCRAFT

What does this mean?

Fieldcraft is learning to be a good soldier in the open air, and learning how to survive when living in the **field**.

What do soldiers have to learn?

Soldiers have to learn to **camouflage** themselves. They can use anything around them, such as leaves and branches, to make themselves hard to see. They put special dark cream on their faces.

The enemy will be wearing camouflage too, so it is important to learn how to spot them! Recruits are taught to spot body shapes hiding behind bushes or trees.

What does the training involve?

The training can be cold and wet and uncomfortable! A soldier may have to sleep outdoors, and cook food in the open air.

MAP READING

What does this mean?

Soldiers need to be able to read maps so that they know exactly where they are at all times.

What do soldiers have to learn?

The most important thing to learn is not to get lost! When soldiers have learnt how to use maps they learn how to find North without using a compass. They can use the stars at night and shadows during the day to do this.

What does the training involve?

Soldiers may use **orienteering** as a good way to learn to read maps. More experienced soldiers might be dropped in the field with a map. They are not told where they are. They have to use a map to find their way back to the camp.

WEAPON TRAINING

What does this mean?

Weapon training teaches recruits about guns and other weapons. They need to know how to look after their weapons, how to aim and fire them, and how to use them safely.

What do soldiers have to learn?

The first thing they learn is safety. When a gun is loaded, it must never be pointed anywhere except at the fieldcraft.

Recruits learn how to take a rifle to pieces and put it back together, and how to keep it clean. If a bullet jams in a gun, they need to know how to get it sorted out quickly.

What does the training involve?

As well as learning about guns, recruits will spend a lot of time working on their **marksmanship** – learning how to aim, fire and hit the **target**.

FIRST AID AND DEFENCE

What does this mean?

First aid means helping people who are injured or ill. When soldiers are fighting, it is not always easy to get injured people to hospital or to a doctor.

Soldiers may be hurt by **radiation** from **nuclear weapons**, or by **chemicals and germs** used as weapons.

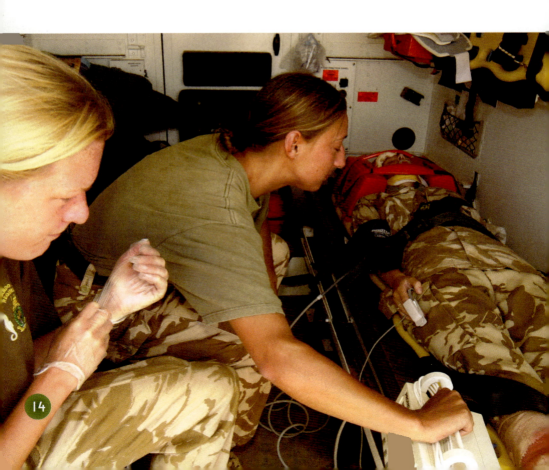

What do soldiers have to learn?

It is important to learn first aid, as this can save lives. When more than one soldier is injured, it is important to work out which person is the most badly hurt. Then that person can be treated first.

Soldiers must also learn to protect themselves from danger with special clothing and breathing equipment.

What does the training involve?

Recruits will learn in a classroom, and by acting out real situations. Sometimes they will practise in a **gas chamber**.

RECREATION AND INITIATIVE TRAINING

What does this mean?

Recreation is what you can do in your spare time such as sports or hobbies. Being a recruit is hard work, but there is time to have fun as well!

Using your initiative means being able to think for yourself and decide what to do without asking someone else.

What do soldiers have to learn?

Soldiers have to learn all sorts of new skills. Most importantly, they have to learn to think for themselves, and be part of a team.

What does the training involve?

Recruits may take part in sport, such as football. They might try other outdoor activities such as canoeing, swimming or **parachuting**.

MILITARY EDUCATION AND WELFARE ADVICE

What do soldiers have to learn?

Soldiers will learn about the rules of life in the army and something about the history of their regiment.

What does 'welfare advice' mean?

New soldiers need advice on any problems they might have. These might be problems with dealing with money, family situations or just feeling homesick.

OFFICER TRAINING

Some recruits want to become officers. First they must do their basic training, which is the same for all soldiers. Then officer cadets must learn how to become a good leader. They must learn how to look after the soldiers that they are in charge of. They will also have to learn about the place of the army in the world and the sorts of work the army has to do.

Becoming an officer is tough – officer cadets are expected to be even fitter than the other recruits!

SPECIAL TRAINING

What jobs can you do in the army?

When recruits have finished their basic training, they can train for a special job. There are hundreds to choose from. They could learn to:

- work with computers or special weapons
- look after equipment
- drive tanks
- help to look after the **stores**
- operate radios
- fly helicopters
- cook the hundreds of meals that an army camp needs every day.

Glossary

attention standing straight, with feet together

camouflage making yourself difficult to see

chemicals and germs weapons that kill by poisoning people or making them ill

field anywhere outside the camp that a soldier works or fights

gas chamber a room that is sealed up and used for experiments with gas, or dangerous germs and chemicals

keeping in step marching together so that everyone's feet and arms move at the same time

marksmanship skill at hitting a target with a gun

nuclear weapons weapons that work by splitting atoms or joining them together. They make huge explosions and give out dangerous rays

orienteering a sport. You must find your way round a special route using a map and going as fast as you can

parachuting jumping from an aircraft with a parachute

quick march marching at a steady, fixed pace

radiation dangerous rays given off by nuclear weapons and the materials used to make them

rifle army gun with a long barrel

stand at ease standing in a more relaxed way, with feet apart

stores the place the army keeps all the things it needs, such as food and ammunition

target what you are aiming at